Building a New House

Everything You Need to Know About How to Build a House with Tips & Advice from Two Licensed Architects (Mother & Daughter)

Table of Contents

Introduction

First, we want to thank you for purchasing this book, and we want you to know that our primary goal in writing this is to help you navigate the complicated process of planning for and building a new home.

Building a house is a common dream that many people share. We all want to live in a customized space that's designed completely around our every desire. Lots of people think that building a home is a fairly simple process, whereas others (those who are more realistic) realize that it is often a long, challenging, and daunting task. Most of us have heard stories of projects-gone-wrong, and we're here to tell you that unfortunately problem projects happen all the time.

In this book, we'll walk you through the steps of this complicated journey to put you on the right track, outlining the entire process so you'll know generally what to expect. We'll also give you plenty of tips to avoid common pitfalls that cause suffering and anguish for many people going through this process. (There is actually a show out there called "Catch a Contractor" you know.) If you're a DIY-er (Do It Yourself-er), then you'll probably need much more than this guide, but at least this is a good starting point for anyone even remotely considering jumping into a home building adventure.

The journey of building your house will ultimately be an experience unlike any other that, if done right, you will absolutely treasure and look back upon with fondness. You'll learn a lot, meet some really interesting and talented craftsmen, and then you will live to appreciate your spectacularly customized home more than others appreciate theirs, because yours was created through your own vision, blood, sweat, and tears. You will have stories, memories, and hard evidence of a tremendous undertaking and accomplishment unlike any other.

Before we get started, we just want to point out that, yes, a lot of the information presented in this book is catered towards informing you about the typical role of an Architect during the process of designing and constructing a new home. However, our intention for going into such detail about that isn't necessarily to convince you to hire an Architect (although of course that would be a good idea). Rather, the purpose is to help you make an informed decision regarding how to proceed, and to help you understand what bases you'll need to find a way to cover on your own should you choose *not* to hire an Architect.

To clarify that point a little further: We're not trying to get you to hire us. Or any Architect for that matter. And we're not trying to toot our own horn, so to speak. But we do think you should at least know how an Architect typically looks out for and protects a Homeowner during construction as part of the normal "checks and balances" system that's built in to the process. This way, if you choose not to hire an Architect, you'll at least better understand what to pay attention to so that you can better protect yourself.

Preface – About Us (Mother + Daughter)

Mother is a Licensed Architect, practicing in South Carolina.

Daughter is a Licensed Architect, practicing in California.

Mother is a practiced traditionalist, and due to the preferences of clients has designed many traditional-style homes throughout rural South Carolina. Mother's aesthetic language is broad and continually evolving.

Daughter tends to prefer the modern style, and has designed many modern homes in California. Conversely, Daughter also greatly appreciates and has a background in Historic Preservation.

Mother designed and built her own (traditional/eclectic-style) house in 1982. This is where Daughter grew up and spent the first 13 years of her life (with Mother, Father, and Son).

Daughter designed and built her own (modern-style) house in 2009 where she still lives today. This home was featured in

Dwell Magazine and Architectural Record, and she was even invited to speak about it at the LA Convention Center and on National Public Radio.

Mother and Daughter have never practiced Architecture together, but frequently consult with one another.

Daughter decided to write this book to help those who share the dream to improve their quality of life by building their own home, but couldn't imagine writing it without Mother's contribution.

Mother nor Daughter claim to be legal or insurance experts. For any information or advice herein regarding these matters, we strongly recommend that you consult with an appropriate professional.

Chapter 1 – Selecting a Site and Obtaining a Survey

Selecting where you want to live is a really big deal that requires lots of research and careful consideration. We always hear the most important factor is "location, location, location," but unfortunately all of us can't afford the beachfront lot or an estate property in the Hamptons. Most of us have to balance "location, location, location" with "budget, budget, budget." Do not overlook the importance of selecting a community where you feel secure and happy though. Time spent becoming familiar with the real estate market in the area is time well spent! Even then, your final property choice will potentially include numerous compromises.

One must carefully consider what impact site selection will have on potential resale value, especially if length of ownership is somewhat in limbo. Take the time and effort to investigate the neighborhood demographics, such as median age, median household income, and average property value, so you'll better understand the future incline or decline of your pending investment. Consider the strength of local schools, as this may also impact your satisfaction and value. Substantial statistical information regarding neighborhoods and school districts can be obtained online. Among countless other websites, www.city-data.com is one of our favorites.

Other important considerations include convenience to work, shopping, recreation, and schools. A short commute will result in tremendous savings of time and treasure over the years if you plan to live in your dream house for quite a while. Look for neighborhoods that are emerging, and where you can count on property values increasing over time. Try to avoid neighborhoods on the decline, even if lots in these neighborhoods are priced lower than lots in up and coming areas.

Does the site provide significant natural views that you want to capture? Or will you carefully create new vistas inside your beautifully landscaped garden wall? What is the neighborhood architectural vernacular, and how does the common thread of materials and styles mesh with your aesthetic taste?

How will local property taxes impact your property choice and reoccurring annual budget? What should you expect to pay for plan review, permit fees, and utility connections in your chosen community? Will codes, ordinances, covenants and restrictions severely limit what can be built on this home site? Some of these Code issues are discussed later in Chapter 6.

Is the site you are considering easily buildable? To answer this question you'll need to understand soil conditions, which is discussed later in Chapter 7. What topographic implications does the site manifest? Is the land relatively flat, or steeply sloped? Is the site large enough to accommodate required parking and vehicular turn around space?

Is there an existing building that must be demolished? Is the building historically significant or could it contain asbestos or lead paint that would require careful and costly disposal? These and other environmental issues should be thoughtfully investigated, often during due diligence period – the time between entering into a contract for sale and closing on the property. Be sure you make the effort and allow the time to thoroughly understand these issues prior to closing.

Due diligence is also a great time to thoroughly investigate existing site infrastructure, such as the availability of underground or overhead electrical power, proximity and size of water and sewer lines, gas lines, telephone, cable, and other fiber optic and wireless communications. Pay attention to the condition of the roads in the neighborhood. If the pavement appears to be in a deteriorated state, check with the City, County, or State Department of Transportation as to when repairs or resurfacing will occur. If the roads belong to a neighborhood association, be sure you understand this financial liability and potential assessment.

When you've finally committed to purchase a property, an updated survey is sometimes a required element of the legal transaction, especially if a lender is involved. When commissioning a property survey for real estate closing, one typically contracts for a minimal boundary line survey. You may want to request from the Surveyor, an additional itemized proposal that could provide more useful information that will save you time and money later on your road to construction. If location, cutting, or trimming trees is a consideration, you will likely benefit from a tree survey. If the site has slope or drainage concerns, a topographic survey will be extremely useful. If you're not sure exactly where the power, water, sewer, gas, etc. are located near or on your site, a utility survey is what you'll need to move forward with design. If you combine tree, topographic, and/or utility surveys with the boundary survey required to complete your property purchase, you'll have essential site information at your fingertips when you move forward with designing your new home.

Chapter 2 – Redefining an Architect

Most people think of an Architect as the creative type, who hunches over a sketch pad for hours a day dreaming up amazing fancy new designs, specifically focused on aesthetic appeal. I probably would have thought that too, if not for growing up with a parent as an Architect. Although creating and sketching is part of our job, these tasks are merely a small piece of the entire puzzle. An Architect is more your tour guide and advisor throughout the entire process. Architects tend to be good at understanding the big-picture process of putting the puzzle together, while at the same being able to hone in and focus on the smallest of details. Also, we must be adept at the technical nature of building construction and performance, while maintaining the creative vision of the end-result at the same time. The word "Architect" originally comes from the meaning "Master Builder". However, we really see Architecture more as "the Art of Balance".

Here are all the things an Architect typically does:

1. Your Architect can help you choose (or 'vet') a Site if your site has not already been selected.

2. Your Architect will help you find reputable Consultants your project may require, from the beginning of the process to the end. This may include a Surveyor, a Geotechnical Engineer, a Structural Engineer, etc. Architects not only have lots of experience and contacts within the industry, but are usually tremendously resourceful by nature.

3. Your Architect will do all the Code Research for your property to determine what you are allowed to build, where you can build it, how big or tall it can be, etc.

4. Your Architect will communicate with you, asking questions, taking notes, and pushing you to delve deeper than you even imagined, just to gain a complete understanding of your project goals and objectives. He/she will create a "Program" and "Scope" as a guide or checklist to ensure you're all on the same page as to what specifically will be achieved.

5. Your Architect will then come up with several rounds and iterations of design options specific to your project, and present and review these design schematics with you, in search of establishing what you like the best.

6. Your Architect will turn this schematic vision into a set of technical Drawings that will be used for Contractor Bidding, Agency Permitting, and ultimately for Construction.

7. Your Architect will assist you in the Agency Permitting process, often times by visiting the various regulatory agencies and submitting the drawings herself.

8. Your Architect will assist you in the Bidding Phase, usually by helping you send out the "Requests for Proposals" to various qualified Contractors, then by helping you compare the Bids, in an Apples-to-Apples format, to see which Contractor is right for your project.

9. Your Architect will even help you determine what form of Contract is best for your project, and will review the Contract before you sign with the Contractor.

10. During Construction, your Architect will visit the jobsite at regular intervals to observe the quality of work, and will keep you informed as to whether or

not the Contractor's built work is in compliance with his Contract and with the Drawings.

11. Your Architect will also be available to answer the Contractor's questions; help you initiate any design changes that may occur during Construction; and will review any Change Order Requests submitted by the Contractor to determine whether or not these are legitimate increases or fair credits for work scope reductions.

12. Your Architect will protect your interests by reviewing all Contractor invoices ("Applications for Payment") and in many cases will require the Contractor to revise to prevent over-billing, or billing ahead of schedule.

13. Your Architect will also help facilitate the Close-Out process to bring the project to full completion, wrapping up any loose ends with the paperwork or on the jobsite.

Whew! After reading this list, has your understanding changed regarding exactly what an Architect will contribute to your project?

Chapter 3 – Deciding Whether or Not to Hire an Architect

Before you can decide whether or not to hire an Architect, it's important to first consider the benefits of having one on your team.

You may be wondering whether or not it's required by Code to hire an Architect for your project. That's a hard question to answer because simply put: "It depends." Each municipality in each state has its own set of regulations on this topic, so if you're really still on the fence about whether or not you want to hire an Architect, just give your local building department a call, and ask!

However, after reading the above list enumerating all the activities an Architect will handle for you, we are confident that you understand the value that a skilled Architect will add to your project.

Here are some of the tangible benefits:

1.   Your home will be better-designed and therefore ultimately more valuable

2. You will have the benefit of a trusted guide and advisor throughout the process with lots of experience in the industry

3. The drawings provided by the Architect will provide a basis for various Contractors to Bid on the EXACT SAME SCOPE. Therefore the Bids will be much easier to compare "apples to apples"

4. The Architect can help you review the Contractors' Bids during the Bidding Phase, and will likely help save you money and/or limit Change Orders down the road. See Chapter 12 for how this works.

5. The Architect operates on your behalf during Construction, checking to see that the Construction is in accordance with the level of quality expected and agreed to in the Contract.

6. All Change Orders and Payments to the Contractor are reviewed first by the Architect to establish whether or not the figures are legitimate and correct. Both of us have had numerous experiences where we believe we saved Clients as much money as our entire Architectural fee through these reviews!

Chapter 4 – What Qualities to Look For

So let's assume by now that you've decided to hire an Architect. What qualities are important to look for, and how can you compare one Architect to the next? This really is a personal decision, and you'll probably want to choose the Architect you feel most comfortable with, but here are more tips on good qualities to look for in an Architect:

Someone who Listens and Asks Questions. You want to find an Architect who will take the time to really listen to what you're saying, and asks follow-up questions to get clarification and a deeper understanding. This is important because it's absolutely critical that the Architect you work with knows exactly what you're trying to achieve. Even if you're not the best at verbalizing, your Architect should know how to ask the right questions to get the information out of you. It's our job to understand your goals so that we can work towards achieving them.

Someone who Communicates Effectively. You want to find an Architect who not only listens well, but can also explain things effectively and easily. When an Architect can explain or describe something to you clearly, you'll feel more confident that he/she knows exactly what you meant and that you're all on the same page. This will relieve anxiety during the process.

Someone with at least some Field Experience. We think it's best to find an Architect who has a least some field experience. It's easy as an Architect to draw something on paper or on our computer, without a thorough understanding of how it actually gets built on the jobsite. This type of disconnect is something you should try to avoid. You'll want to ask whether or not he/she has any hands-on field experience in Construction, or at the very least, how frequently he/she visits the jobsites of other construction projects and what types of things he/she looks for while there.

Someone who can Balance or Unify Competing Objectives. In designing and building a home, there are often competing objectives. For example, you want your house to look incredible and magnificent! But on the other hand, you probably are on a budget, right? Finding an Architect who not only understands, but also commiserates with your conflict and can actually use the budget or other constraint or challenge to inspire a creative solution that looks magnificent – now that's turning lemons into lemonade! You want an Architect with that "can-do" mindset.

Someone without a Design Ego. There are many Architects out there who, if you hire them, will basically use your commission and construction budget as an opportunity to build another monument to themselves. The dwelling won't truly be designed for you. It will be designed for the cover of their new book. Stay away from these ego-centric Architects, and find somebody who wants to make your dream come true, not their own. Or better yet, someone whose dream IS to help you make your dream come true. A win-win.

Chapter 5 – The Process of Hiring an Architect

Hiring an Architect is a relatively easy process. First you contact the Architect (or several) and meet with them, preferably at your home site, to discuss the project. Usually there's no charge for this initial meeting, but it's best to ask when first contacting them. Then the Architect will put together a "Proposal for Services" which will generally describe his/her understanding of what the scope of services will be for your project. The proposal may be listed by Phase, with a description of each Phase, and an estimated dollar figure associated with each Phase and a Total at the end. There's often a place for your "Acceptance of Proposal" at the bottom of the last sheet.

Once the Proposal is signed by both Client and Architect, the Architect will submit a formal Contract (Owner-Architect Agreement) for you to review and sign. Many architects use a standard AIA (American Institute of Architects) form. Even using the Standard Contract, we always recommend that you read thoroughly, review it carefully, and if you still have questions or concerns, then you can always contact your attorney for advice.

It's important to note that different Architects may present you with different types of fee structures. Some will want to be paid by the hour, whereas others will provide you with a lump sum for each phase, and yet others will want to be paid as a fixed percentage of the total construction cost. There are clear advantages and disadvantages to each (for both you and the Architect), so it really just comes down to figuring out which structure you and your Architect are mutually most comfortable with.

Chapter 6 – Code Research

After you've selected a site and hired an Architect, next is the research phase, with the intention of determining what is allowed to be built in accordance with the various Codes and regulations of any Agencies having jurisdiction. A good place to go for an initial inquiry is your local building department. Generally, you'll be dealing with two types of Codes, possibly three or even four. If you're working with an Architect, the Architect will do all the research for you, or because of his/her familiarity with the locale the need for research will be limited. Your architect will succinctly summarize the options you are allowed to build.

Code Type #1:

The local Zoning Code (also sometimes known as the Municipal Code or Planning Code).The purpose of the local Zoning Code is to regulate the patterns of land development by area. For example, you wouldn't want someone to build a skyscraper in your small residential neighborhood on a cul-de-sac, would you? The Zoning Code creates and defines districts or neighborhoods based on predominant types of land use in that specific area, to create consistency and uniformity. District types include things like Residential (distinguishing Single Family vs. Multi-Family Residential apartment buildings or condominiums, Industrial, Agricultural, Commercial, etc.)Thus, one of the first things you'll need to verify with the Zoning Code is that you're allowed to build a house (known as "Single Family

Residential") in the area where you own or are purchasing land.

Assuming you are allowed to build a house, the next data you'll need to determine from the Zoning Code are maximum building height; maximum number of stories allowed; front yard setback (distance from the front yard's property line to the front wall of your house); side yard setback (distance from the side yard property line); and rear yard setback (the minimum distance required from your rear property line to the rear wall of your house).

The Zoning Code also will provide information regarding projections - if, and how much, you are allowed to "project" into these yards (front, side, and rear) with building elements such as balconies, canopies, roof edges and eaves, bay windows, chimneys, etc. Generally speaking, researching the Zoning Code will eventually provide the shape of the allowable building "envelope" in which you can build. Think of it as an invisible 3-dimensional box that you can't build beyond. Of course you don't have to use all that space!

Code Type #2:

The local Building Code (also known as "Building and Safety"). This code is usually adopted from, and sometimes further amended from, the State Building Code, which is adopted from, and sometimes amended from, the International Building Code or IBC. The purpose of this Code is to create a set of minimum requirements for built structures, ensuring that what's being built is safe for the building's Occupants, Visitors or Guests, and also surrounding Neighbors. The Building Code dictates rules regarding type of construction in terms of structural requirements and types of materials (fire resistance, etc.). It also takes into account safety by setting standards for elements such as how steep stairs can be. For example, you can't use a ladder in a house to get from the main living floor up to the bedroom floor, right? You also can't have stairs that are too steep. The building code actually specifies the minimum number of inches that the tread must be, and the maximum number of inches that the riser (vertical part of each step) can be. Also the handrail location, type, size, attachment, and structural capacity are part of the requirements set forth by the Building Code. The examples listed herein are really just the tip of the iceberg! The Building Code is a pretty hefty read. If you're working with an Architect, he/she will already be generally familiar with the requirements.

Code Type #3:

If you've chosen a neighborhood with its own design requirements, you may be subject to comply with CC&Rs (Covenants, Conditions, and Restrictions), which are regulated by a local Design Review Board. Neighborhood requirements are a matter you should have been advised about when you bought property in the neighborhood, and this information is typically included in your Real Estate

Transaction Purchase. As an example of a CC&R requirement, a neighborhood may require that all houses must be of a particular architectural style, or spatial massing, or use certain color combinations. In this case, you'll have to comply with these requirements and submit your plans to the Board for their review, comment and approval.

Code Type #4:

Occasionally, there will be some other miscellaneous code that may apply, based on the specifics of where you choose to live (as if the above three codes aren't enough, right?!?). It's difficult to prognosticate what this fourth code could be, but examples include some we've previously encountered such as "Hillside Ordinance" if your project site is on sloped property with topographical contours (AKA "not very flat" land). In this case, there may be additional standards you must comply with, depending on your municipality's regulations. These types of regulations are often adopted by the Building Code or Zoning Code, so it may already be covered in Code Types 1 or 2. Another example would be a property is in a Historic District or Historic Zone. Then, you'll need to comply with certain "compatibility" requirements to maintain the character of the neighborhood. Again, there's usually a review board with a handful of members that will look over your plans and give their opinion and recommendation for approval or denial.

In any case, whatever the Code requirements are that regulate what you can or cannot build on your land, it's always best to fully understand the options, opportunities, and limitations in advance. In far too many instances, we see wasted time and effort when people have not done their research, yet they begin planning what they want to build without looking into exactly what they're allowed to build first.

If you're not up for this vast amount of research yourself, hiring an Architect will usually save you a lot of time and effort. The Codes are often very complex and difficult to read or fully understand. Codes are written in technical, legal, and construction industry jargon, and often open to multiple interpretations. Therefore it's a good idea to have someone well equipped and experienced to assist you.

Chapter 7 – Geotechnical Investigation

Depending where your project is located, your site may or may not require a Geotechnical Investigation and Soils Report as part of your local Building Department submission. Again, the best course of action is to find out in advance as part of the Code Research phase. A call or visit to your local building department is a great starting point. Simply provide an accurate physical property address, and ask whether their knowledge of the area indicates that a Soils Report for their approval may be required when drawings are submitted for Plan Check.

If you are indeed required to submit a Soils Report, you'll need to get a Geotechnical Engineer on board early in the project. The soils investigation sometimes requires drilling and soil-sampling for laboratory testing. The Geotechnical Engineer will write a report that includes information regarding your site's soil load-resisting capacities, and the report may also include recommendations for the building's foundation structural system.

42

Chapter 8 – Understanding the Programming Phase

Programming is a fancy term for an orderly review and synopsis of elements you want to include in the project's scope. For example, it can be as simple as wanting an Entry Space, a Formal Living Room, Kitchen, Dining Room, Two Bedrooms, and Two Baths.

A better way to think of Programming though, is an opportunity to consider how you like to move throughout your house and the way you function in your house during the day, the night, and on weekends. Think about what you like to do in the house, and where you like to do it, etc. For example: When you get home, where's the first place you go? Do you go to the kitchen to pull a beer from the fridge? Would you like to sip a cup of coffee in the kitchen while peering out the window? Or do you go straight to the couch and turn on the TV? Do you head to your computer to check your email? Or do you attempt to avoid your desk area because sitting there brings on guilt over unfinished work or unpaid bills?

Another example: Do you shop for all your groceries once a week, arriving home with your arms absolutely loaded down with grocery bags? In that case, conveniently locating the kitchen in close proximity to the garage and minimizing the walk distance for unloading your heavy packages may be an important priority for your new dream home.

Yet another example: Do you have (or are you planning on having) young children, and you'd like their bedrooms to be nearby yours so you can keep an ear out for a crying baby. Or on the contrary, do you have a drum-playing teenager who you want to be on the far side of the house?

And one more example: Are you an avid reader? Do you read during the day? Or at night? If you like to read on the weekend mornings, maybe you'd like a comfy bench in front of the east-facing window; however, if you're more of a night-owl reader, maybe you'll need a good spotlight above your bed.

We could go on and on with examples, but do you get the idea?

This exercise may sound silly and too simple, but the deeper you force yourself to think about your habits, tendencies, and preferences, the more customized your house will become. Hopefully your successful programming phase will lead to a home that really fits you like a glove.

At the end of the Programming Phase, your goal is to have a written succinct-but-complete bullet point list of all your goals, objectives, and requirements. Whether one page or fifteen pages, your Program should be so clear that you could hand it to anyone, and the reader would instantly know you as if he or she had been living with you for years. Yes, all houses have a living room, a kitchen, bedrooms and bathrooms; but no two person's or families' lists would be the same! This is what will ultimately make your house truly YOURS.

Also, the Programming Phase is a good time to begin to define your Schedule and Budget.

Schedule: It is extremely common for a construction project to take longer than expected, so it's prudent to pick a realistic timeframe that is easily achievable, but also incorporates a little bit of "cushion". You don't want to put yourself in a situation where you're living in a hotel during construction intended to take exactly 6 months, without being prepared with funds set aside for a 7th and possibly 8th month in the hotel, if circumstances require.

Budget: Much like the schedule, cost overruns are not uncommon. So while you have a project Budget in mind (whether by dollar-per-square-foot, or overall project cost), it is imperative to set aside a 'Contingency' Fund of 20%-25%. This will be discussed again in Chapter 13.

Chapter 9 – The Design Phase

This is the Phase of the project that most people really get excited about when they first begin dreaming of building their own home. And for good reason, the design process is really quite fun! If you're not an Architect, and you haven't hired one yet, we highly recommend getting an Architect on board before tackling this phase alone. A distinct difference in quality is readily apparent when a professional Architect is involved in the design, and the overall value of your home will certainly be increased. Designing a house (or any structure for that matter) truly is an art form. Unless you are a creative out-of-the-box thinker, balanced with a pragmatic and scientific side, combined and capped off with organizational and problem-solving skills, who also has the technical experience of piecing a home together, then your dream deserves that you engage someone with all these character traits and skills: an Architect.

Designing your home incorporates everything we've discussed so far. All of the fuzzy, difficult issues begin to morph and eventually merge into a fantastic vision. Specific Site Conditions (direction of the property's best views, solar orientation to maximize daylighting, etc.); the Code requirements that you researched (Chapter 6); and your Programming objectives (Chapter 8) are all blended together in this process. If done well, all these criteria will essentially be transformed into character-defining and customizing features. A good Designer can really see the big picture, taking all of your program elements into consideration, and sometimes producing several possible scenarios to achieve your objectives all wrapped up with a pretty bow. Speaking from experience, some of our best projects resulted from the most challenging and restrictive circumstances. Architecture can certainly be the science of turning lemons into lemonade.

When working with an Architect, you can expect (or request) that he/she present several different schematic design solutions, each different from the others, that you will review and discuss together. Then, you will either outright select one of the choices to move forward with, or you may appreciate certain features of each one and request that your favorite aspects all be meshed together into a new design solution. In any case, the design process continually gets refined as decisions are made, and the specifics become more and more detailed. You and your Architect are operating as a Team during this phase, and often a real bond develops as you piggy-back ideas off of one another, coming up with things that neither of you could have thought of without the other. The process is enjoyable for both you and the Architect. As you complete the design process, you are both proud of the design you share, and you are both very excited to move forward into construction in order to bring your shared vision to reality.

Chapter 10 – Drawing Preparation

Once all the major design decisions have been established, your Architect will need some time to create a set of detailed Construction Drawings that define the full scope of work to any Bidding Contractor, to the Agencies reviewing the Drawings, and ultimately to the Contractor who is selected to build your house. The drawings must be fully developed, detailed, and thorough. Ultimately, you and your contractor will sign the Contract for Construction, which is directly linked to this set of Construction Drawings. Information missing from the drawings can potentially create an avenue for dispute and potential Change Order expense and delay down the road. Therefore, patience is in your best interest. Do not to put too much pressure on flying through this phase. Give your Architect the reasonable amount of time required to complete this task.

At this point in your project, your Architect has likely recommended other Consultants whose input is needed for your project, for example a Structural Engineer (depending on the Code requirements, location of site, and type of Structure). In this scenario, during this phase, the Architect will be "coordinating" the different drawing sets, and combining the Structural Drawings with the Architectural Drawings to create one complete set of Drawings. This 'coordination' also takes time, so be patient with this process also.

Chapter 11 – Agency Permitting

Permitting often occurs simultaneous with Bidding (Chapter 12), but for the purposes of explaining distinct processes, we've written separate chapters. Keep in mind that time can be saved by submitting the drawings to the regulatory agency for review and permitting, and on the following day you can issue the same set of drawings to several Contractors, requesting Bids.

This Chapter is dedicated to Permitting, so let's jump right into it. In all likelihood there are several Codes you may be required to observe and comply with, your local agencies probably have this process streamlined, wherein submitting the drawings to one department will trigger review by another department or departments. Best practice is to inquire directly with your local building agency to learn how their process works, and to also better understand the possible time required by the permitting process.

When the Drawings are ready and complete (Chapter 10), your architect may assist you by delivering the Drawings to the building department and submitting for what's called "Plan Check". Generally, Plan Check includes filling out an application, paying a fee, and then leaving the roll of drawings with the building department for several weeks for staff to review and write comments regarding. When the plan review process is complete, your Architect will retrieve the drawings from the building department, and he or she will revise the Construction Drawings as required and respond to the "Plan

Check Corrections." Rest assured, this is a normal process, and does not imply that anything is wrong. Your Architect will spend a few days or weeks (whatever it takes) to address the comments or corrections noted by the building department "Plan Check Engineer" and then he/she will resubmit a revised set of drawings for a second round of review. This may be the final round, though if the project is complicated or unique, there may be several rounds of comments and revisions. Once this process is complete, the department will notify you or your Architect that the permit is "Ready to Issue." At that point, you may have selected a Contractor (see Chapters 12 & 13), and the Contractor will go to the building department to retrieve the Permit.

Chapter 12 – Soliciting and Comparing Bids from Contractors

Bidding is a process that appears fairly simple, but often complexities are overlooked and problems occur down the road. Let us explain. You give the drawings to several Contractors, asking each how much building your house will cost. Each contractor responds with a proposed price. After thorough review, you will likely select the Contractor with the lowest price, assuming he/she appears likeable and trustworthy. Right?

WRONG! If you approach Bidding Phase this simply, please expect to have problems during Construction.

Below are some helpful tips to consider during this process:

Pre-Qualify all Contractors you're considering before inviting them to bid on your project.

This means selecting a handful of Contractors, look up their license numbers online (or through your state's Licensing Board) to verify their license is in good standing. Interview each Contractor in depth to determine what kind of work they've done; whether or not they've built a house similar to yours; how many jobs they have ongoing at any one time; etc. Ask for references, and definitely call the references. Speak with former Clients to ask about their experience. Ask to see some of the Contractor's completed work. Ask to see a project site that is currently underway, and carefully observe whether or not the jobsite seems to be adequately staffed, moving swiftly, and clean, orderly, and safety conscious. Ask when the project was started to determine if reasonable progress has been made within that timeframe.

Ask your Architect to Create a Schedule of Values Bid Form, and to help you review the Bids.

Simply put, all Bidding Contractors will receive the exact same bid form with a list of line items, and Blank Spaces to fill in the cost of each individual line item. Using this bid method, you (or your Architect) can create a spreadsheet comparing Apples-to-Apples for each specific individual line item, providing plenty of good intel. For example, imagine that "Bidder A" has $35,000 listed for Windows, "Bidder B" has $36,500 listed for Windows, but "Bidder C" has $12,000 listed for windows. Well, you were just able to identify that "Bidder C" has likely factored something in incorrectly! Now you (or your Architect) can call him or meet with him to ask, "Hey, are you sure you bid that 'Windows' line item correctly? Do you want to revisit the drawings and verify that everything is included?" He will probably get back to you and say "Oh wow, yes, I completely forgot to include the 10 windows on the South Elevation." So if you were originally hoping to go with "Bidder C" because his overall bid seemed low and you thought this would save money, think again. A

58

nasty dispute and eventual Change Order will erupt down the road. Yes, all of the windows would be "legally" included in the Contract and therefore the Contractor would be "legally" required to provide the 10 windows he overlooked. But REALISTICALLY, that would never happen – even if it is his mistake, let us assure you, nothing in Construction is free. Conversely, you can use the same technique to conclude that another Bidder may be over-inflating a particular line item, and possibly offer him an opportunity to re-evaluate that item. Consider having your Architect involved in this process, as a set of experienced eyes on all the numbers is absolutely invaluable!

Consider not only Costs, but Schedule too.

We all know that time is money, and if you're putting yourself up in other digs while you're waiting on your house to be completed, every day the house remains unfinished is another day paying for hotel or other living accommodation expense. Each Bidder may have a different staffing and scheduling approach, so be sure to discuss these matters during the Bid Phase. Perhaps "Bidder A's" bid is slightly less expensive than "Bidder B", but if "Bidder B" can complete the job two months quicker, that time has value that should be factored into the decision equation!

Chapter 13 – Signing the Contract for Construction

As mentioned in the Preface, we are not Attorneys and therefore advise you to consult with an appropriate Contract Attorney during the contract process. However, here are pointers for issues you should at least consider, based on our experience.

Don't Sign the Contractor's Version

We strongly recommend that you do not sign the Contractor's Proposal, or the Contractor's custom version of a Contract without thorough review. The terms and conditions within these documents are often in the Contractor's favor in the event of a dispute, and not in your interest. A neutral version is best, one that is fair for both parties, such as the AIA's A101 + A201 (used in combination). The AIA documents can be purchased at reasonable cost, and these documents typically offer much more protection than a Contractor's custom version of a Construction Contract.

Different options are available for you to choose from as to the type of Contract, in terms of compensation. For example, the A101 document mentioned above is for a "Stipulated Sum" agreement, so going into the project, you will have agreed upon an actual fixed total cost for the completion of the project. This means if the Contractor can finish the project for less money, he keeps the difference as Profit. But if it costs him more money than he expected, he has to come up with the difference.

Another option is a "Cost of the Work Plus a Fee" model, wherein you pay the Contractor for all the materials and labor, and additionally pay an agreed-upon percentage for overhead and profit. This can be arranged to have a "Guaranteed Maximum Price" or without a "Guaranteed Maximum Price."

There are advantages and disadvantages of each model, so the type of Contract you choose really is up to your own preference, based on what you and your Contractor are most comfortable with. You should research the options further on the AIA website, and talk to your attorney for more advice.

Have a Contingency Fund

Whichever Contract type you choose, in any case, it's imperative to include and account for an additional Contingency amount of typically 20%-25%. You don't necessarily have to let the Contractor know about this, although it's common for a Contractor to encourage this as well. The Contingency is simply for unforeseen or unpredictable circumstances, and is sometimes difficult to explain to those just starting this process. While of course we all hope it isn't needed, it's certainly a possibility that this cushion will come in handy and you'll be glad you had accounted for it and set aside the extra funds. The worst case scenario that we're trying to avoid is you start the construction process believing it will cost X amount, then something happens or changes are made, and now it actually costs 20% more, and then you have to stop construction because you don't have the money. Think of it like traveling… if you go on vacation, you may have factored in the plane flight, hotel, meals, etc., even down to the little things like bus fare. But little unexpected expenses can still sneak up on you, for example maybe your bus didn't show up on time and you had to pay for a taxi. You wouldn't go on vacation to a foreign country without a little extra cushion "just in case" money, would you? It's important to be able to afford to roll with the punches if and when they occur. And the good news is, if the punches never do occur, you'd be part of the elite minority of home builders where everything goes right, and you'll be the talk of the town! Consider it a blessing and a bonus. But do not expect it.

Tie the Contract to your Drawings, but not to the Contractor's Proposal

Be sure your Contract specifically references the drawings that you and your Architect worked so hard to put together. The Contract should explicitly list every single drawing sheet, referencing the page number and the date on the page. This way, it's very clear what the specific scope of work the

Contractor is responsible for completing. You don't want to constantly hear things like "That toilet wasn't included in my bid, so it's now a Change Order" do you? No, you want to be able to point to that cute little plan-view drawing of the toilet and say "Yes, it was in your bid. Here it is in the Drawings on sheet A2.04. And your Contract specifically states that you're responsible for complying with the drawings including sheet A2.04." Take that!

On that same note, it's typically best to avoid referencing the Contractor's Proposal within the Contract for Construction. This way, you avoid any confusing about a certain requirement being on the drawings but not in the proposal. Instead it will be clear that the Drawings govern, and his Proposal does not.

Require your Contractor to have Insurance

Again, we are most certainly not Insurance experts, therefore we highly recommend that you consult with your Insurance Agent for advice regarding specifically what types of coverage and limits your Contractor should be responsible for carrying. Types to consider and discuss with your agent include: General Liability Insurance, Workers Compensation Insurance, Automobile Insurance, etc. Also, you as a property owner should consider having your own Course of Construction (AKA "Builder's Risk") insurance. Please get all this advice from your local Insurance Expert. Also ask about which policies you should require that your Contractor list you as an "Additional Insured."

Chapter 14 – The Construction Phase & Contractor Payments

If you've followed all our advice so far, the Construction phase has the potential to go smoothly. You should have a Qualified Contractor, whose Bid was based on thorough set of Drawings and vetted by you and your Architect, and you should have a solid Contract with a high degree of Owner protection.

There are a few different components to the Construction Process that you may want to be aware of. All of these processes should be discussed within your Contract for Construction, and it's really important to become familiar with how the Contract delegates responsibilities for these issues. The following information may vary according the Contract you signed, but will give you a general understanding of the way things work.

Giving the Contractor a Deposit

States have different laws on making deposits for construction, but often times they limit the Contractor's request for a deposit to 10% or less. In general, you shouldn't need to make a deposit for uncompleted work; Part of the Contractor's job is to be able to fund the project, being paid only after having made progress. If anything, you may need to pay for certain materials that the Contractor needs to order to get started. In that case, certainly pay no more than 50% and require proof in advance that the materials will be ordered in your name and will be delivered to your jobsite or an agreed-upon storage facility. You can even suggest to pay upon delivery. Never pay a deposit blindly without fully understanding what you're paying for, and how you'll get it. It's always a good idea to become familiar with your state's laws regarding deposits for Construction. And don't be afraid to raise an eyebrow if your Contractor asks for a lot of money upfront.

When it's Time to Make a Payment

It's true that the best way to keep your project's Construction moving swiftly is to pay on time; but certainly not before the work is done (to the expected and agreed-upon level of quality). This is how the process works: The Contractor will submit an "Application for Payment" that breaks down his request for money for each individual line item, and assigns a percentage of completion. Your Architect will review the Application for Payment (ACP) and may request some revisions if he/she is not in agreement on the percentage of work completed. Once your Architect is comfortable with the ACP, he/she will submit it to you, stating that "to the best of his/her knowledge", the work for which the Contractor's requesting payment is complete in accordance with the Contract. Then, you review it to your satisfaction, then you write the check. Your Contract may have a provision for withholding Retainage, so it's common that you'll only pay 90% (for example) of what's complete, withholding the remaining 10% until the final completion of the project.

Mechanic's Lien Laws

This is one of the most difficult topics to explain, yet one of the most important for you to understand. Each state has different Lien Laws, so we will keep this description general, and we strongly encourage you to do more research or speak to an Attorney to gain a better understanding of your state's Lien Laws. Having this understanding may prevent Construction-gone-wrong issues, for example when you pay the Contractor, but the Contractor fails to pay his Subcontractor, then the Subcontractor comes after you looking for his money, and files a Lien on your property.

The purpose of a Lien Law really is to protect a Subcontractor or Vendor that supplied material or labor to improve your property in some way. Because your Contract is only with the Contractor, and you do not have a direct Contract with the Subcontractors, this is the mechanism for their protection.

You may be wondering, how does this translate into a recommended action that I can take to prevent this from happening?

There are forms called "Lien Releases" (AKA "Lien Waivers" or similar) that you should absolutely require your Contractor to submit (one from each and every Subcontractor during each and every billing cycle, so expect to have a huge pile of them) with every Application for Payment. The first version is called a "Conditional" Release or Waiver, wherein the Subcontractor is essentially saying, and we're paraphrasing here just to get the point across, "If I get paid the X amount I'm owed, then I'll give up my rights to file a lien on your property." Then after you make the payment to the Contractor, when he submits the next Application for Payment, your Contractor should submit "Unconditional" Releases or Waivers from those same Subcontractors that basically express they've been paid by saying, again we're paraphrasing here, "I've already been paid the X amount I was owed, so I am hereby giving up my rights to lien your property."

So, with the first ACP, expect to receive only "Conditional" releases, and for each ACP thereafter, expect to receive both "Conditional" releases and "Unconditional" releases. And if your Contractor isn't submitting these to you, then you may withhold payment until he does. He may whine a little about the extra paperwork, but stand firm and continue requesting it until you get it. It's that important.

Architect Site Visits

It's always a good idea for the Architect to visit the jobsite regularly (once or twice a week if the project is moving along at a nice pace) to become familiar with the progress of the work and observe the quality of work. If he/she notices anything wrong, he/she will let you know, and also will put the Contractor on notice that he needs to correct the mistake immediately. Also these regular site visits keep the Architect familiar with the progress of the work, making it easier to review the Applications for Payment and answer any questions the Contractor may have.

Note: This is the point at which a lot of home owners don't really understand the Architect's function, and if they're paying the Architect hourly for example, all of a sudden the "expense" can seem unnecessary. However, keep in mind that this is the point in the project where the metal meets the road! What's the point of having something worked out in detail on paper if you're not going to ensure that it's being built correctly in the field? And if you think that you can see everything for yourself, so you don't need to pay your Architect to come take a look, then I encourage you to think of it like this: You know how when you get an X-ray at the dentist, your dentist can just take one glance at the X-ray and see a cavity? Yet try as you might, you would never have been able to see it without him pointing it out to you? Yeah, exactly.

Inspections by the "Building Inspector"

You may notice that a government "Building Inspector" drops by your jobsite every now and then, usually at the request of your Contractor after the completion of certain milestones. While the Building Inspector is looking to confirm that certain agency requirements have been met in the construction, he is NOT there on your behalf to ensure the Contractor is complying with your Construction Drawings and Contract.

When the Contractor has a Question

In a formal type of project, the Contractor will officially submit any questions to the Architect on a piece of paper called a "Request for Information" (RFI). Sometimes for small Single Family Residential projects, this process gets reduced down to just sending a quick email with the question, or even sometimes asking in person. In any case, the Architect should aim to respond as quickly as possible with whatever additional information is needed, whether it be a design decision regarding aesthetics, or a new drawing detail describing a certain construction joint. Even if the Contractor has a question that will ultimately need to be answered by the Owner, it's good practice to include or go through the Architect, as these types of changes can often affect other aspects of the Work (schedule, cost, payments) and the Architect needs to be aware of these things.

When there is a Change in Scope

If your Contractor believes that something he's asked to do was not included in your Contract, or was not represented on the Drawings, he may submit a Change Order Request (COR) to you and/or your Architect. You and your Architect will review this COR to determine whether or not it's legitimate, meaning whether or not the Contractor is due additional money to complete this work. If it is legitimately due, then the Architect will issue a Change Order (CO), all three parties will sign the document, and the Contractor proceeds with the work. Change Orders essentially modify your Contract changing the scope, to either increase the Sum, reduce the Sum, increase the Schedule, or reduce the Schedule.

Chapter 15 – How to Finish Strong

The Construction process can be exhausting, and it's a bit like running a marathon. Don't stop early, just short of the finish line. Use the momentum from the project to complete the final details of the house, including any landscaping or site work, and the finishing touches such as any interior decorating you've planned. It's important to recognize that if you don't do it now, the likelihood of it being done later is much smaller, because you won't have the same momentum and drive. Push yourself to finish strong, tongue out, and arms in the air. You may even want to memorialize the moment and the finished work by having the house photographed professionally. You can use these photographs to submit your house to acclaimed design magazines if it's worthy, or use them down the road when you're ready to list your house for sale.

Project Close-Out

Project Close-Out is the process by which you wrap up all the loose ends with your Contractor. Your Contractor will put together a 'Punch List' of work left to be done, then you and your Architect will review the list and add to it. This will better define what's left to do, so that you can all get on the same page as to expectations for how your Contractor must complete the final nit-picky details and finishes. The Punch List will include absolutely everything, even a little scratch on the wall in the hallway you noticed that the Contractor will need to touch-up, or a missing light bulb.

The Contractor is generally responsible for final Clean-Up (assuming it was included in your Contract), so he should leave your house perfectly spotless, even bringing in a specialized clean-up crew if necessary.

Your Contract may require that your Contractor provide a 3-ring binder with User Manuals for any equipment that was installed, and also any applicable Warranties for materials or equipment. If your Contract requires, your Contractor may also turn over any "Attic Stock" items (leftover materials that he didn't use, that you may need to use later for maintenance or repair – for example a box of leftover bathroom tiles, etc.).

Terms often Confused

There are a group of terms that apply to the completion of a project that often get confused with one another. Below we've attempted to define each of them and distinguish among them.

Final Inspection: This is a step required by the building department, wherein the Building Inspector comes out for Final Inspection and signs off on the building department's checklist.

Certificate of Occupancy: This is the document from the building department certifying that a building is in compliance with all applicable codes and therefore suitable for occupancy.

Notice of Completion: This is a document that you may be required to file with the County Recorder's office. It may trigger a tax reassessment, but it also starts the clock for the filing of any Liens on your property (the sooner the clock starts, the sooner it ends!). Also the filing of this document may be required by your lender, if applicable.

Substantial Completion: This is a "term of art" in construction, and relates directly to your Contract. It is a date established by the Architect, on which the house has become "useable" for its intended purposes (to live in). It often establishes the beginning of the Warranty period, and sometimes transfers responsibilities for Insurance and Utilities from the Contractor onto the Owner.

Final Completion: This is another term that relates directly to your Contract for Construction, and established the date that the work is fully complete in accordance with the Contract. Final Payment and the release of Retainage can now be issued.

Conclusion

Thank you again for purchasing this book! We really hope it has shed a little more light on the process of building a new home, and given you information as to how you can prepare and protect yourself along the way.

Undertaking the planning and execution of building a new house can be a daunting but rewarding experience, and if you plan correctly and bring the proper professionals along for the ride, the process can go smoothly and will be quite enjoyable. At the end of it all, you'll have a fantastic place to call home, where you can rest, relax, and recharge, and also invite all your friends over to enjoy and entertain. When it's all said and done, there's really "No Place Like Home" – so why not make it spectacularly customized?

The next step is to just throw yourself into the project, get excited, and get started!

We really hope this book helped to demystify the process for you, and we hope we were able to give you some good advice and perhaps even increase your comfort level a little. So thanks for purchasing this book, and if you found it helpful, we'd greatly appreciate it if you would just take a moment to leave a nice review on Amazon – Thank You!

Made in the USA
Lexington, KY
26 November 2017